Williams & Everett

High Class Paintings

George W. Carmer

Williams & Everett

High Class Paintings
George W. Carmer

ISBN/EAN: 9783337331788

Printed in Europe, USA, Canada, Australia, Japan

Cover: Foto ©Thomas Meinert / pixelio.de

More available books at **www.hansebooks.com**

CATALOGUE

OF

HIGH CLASS PAINTINGS

COLLECTED BY GEORGE W. CARMER
4 East 31st Street, New York.

❧

ON EXHIBITION IN

WILLIAMS & EVERETT'S GALLERIES
190 Boylston Street

From March 9 to March 16, 1899

❧

To be sold by auction
Thursday, March 16th, Friday, March 17th
Evening, 8 o'clock

❧

FRANK A. LEONARD, Auctioneer

Rules and Conditions of Sale.

Paintings and frames sold together.

All bills are due at close of sale.

Pictures to be removed at expense and risk of purchaser.

Pictures not removed on day of sale remain at risk of
purchaser.

No claims allowed after removal of the goods.

Pictures are resold at expense and risk of purchaser.

Deposits must be given when requested.

Purchaser requested to give name and address in full.

Our record of sales in all cases is final.

Orders to buy executed without charge.

FRANK A. LEONARD, *Auctioneer.*

Orders to buy also executed by Williams & Everett,
190 Boylston Street, Boston.

INDEX OF ARTISTS REPRESENTED.

Binet	24
Brownscombe	1
B. S.	6
Boggs	7
Beraud	50
Bradford	54
Brunin	56
Blinks	78, 81
Berne-Bellecour	104
Blommers	106
Bougereau	116
Carradin	25
Chaigneau	35
Corot	44, 71, 96
Casanova	45
Dupré	11, 55, 103
Dennenlin	12
Decamps	18
De Vrindt	79
Diaz	31, 95
Dettè	34, 82
Desgoffe	38
Daubigny	41, 69, 90
Delachaux	61
Edelfelt	2
Eliot	5, 48
Escosura	76
Fulchsel	10
Fonace	9
Fichel	108
Gudin	4
Grant	20
Gerome	85
Gay	117

Hart	. . . .	119, 49, 51
Hobbema	. . . .	94
How	. . . .	97
Haquette	. . . .	98
Hassam	. . . .	102
Henner	. . . .	114
Ireland	. . . . .	62
Israels	. . . .	93
Inness	. . . . .	100
Jettel	. . . . . .	21
Jongkind	. . . .	23, 57, 109
Jacque	. . . . .	40, 89
Kaemmerer	.	101
Laugeè	. . .	64
Lewin	. . . .	19
Lesrel	. . .	8, 67
Monchablon	. . . .	13
McCord	. . . .	28
Michel	. . . . .	29, 107
Monticelli	. . .	30, 75, 111
Mauve	. . . .	37, 86
Madon	. . . . . .	59
Marcotte	. . . . . .	60
Millet	. . . . . .	66
Muller	. . . . .	99
Norton	.	118
Oost	. . ,	110
Perrault	. .	74, 77
Rousseau	. . .	33, 52, 92
Roybet	. . . .	32, 83
Rougeron	. . . .	16
Rix	. . . . .	3
Richet	. . . . .	65
Stevens	. . . . .	14
Schenck	. . . . .	27
Shewin	. . , . , .	54
Semenowsky	. . . .	42, 113
Steinheil	. . . . .	72
Schreyer	. . . . .	91

Troyon .	. 46, 87
Ter Meulin	. 47
Teniers .	, 112
Vibert . .	115
Van Thoren . . .	105
Van Marcke . .	88
Voight . . .	26
Verhas . . .	70
Vely . .	84
Washington .	17
Williems ,	22
Worms . .	39
Wasserman ,	. 43, 68
Wood .	53
Woodwell	58
Wahlberg	. 63, 73
Ziem	. 36, 80
Piot	. 74

Note.

Most of the foreign paintings included in this catalogue were personally secured in Europe; the old pictures from most reliable sources, and the contemporary art from the painters direct or from their business agents.

The entire collection can be relied upon as genuine, and I hereby guarantee every painting as catalogued.

GEORGE W. CARMER.

New York, March 6, '99.

88

AT THE BROOK.

EMIL VAN MARCKE.

CATALOGUE

OF

ᐧPᴁINTINGSᐧ

❧

First Evening Sale

THURSDAY EVENING, MARCH 16th,

8 O'CLOCK.

❧

1

BROWNSCOMBE (J.) . . . Philadelphia

THE WELCOME STEP

41 x 29

2

EDELFELT (A.) . . . . Paris

Pupil of Gerome
Medals, 1880, 1882; Great Gold Medal, 1889; Universal
Exposition and Legion of Honor

"UNDER THE BEECHES"

23¾ x 32⅜

3

RIX (JULIEN) . . . . . New York

FISHERS ISLAND
50 x 30

4

GUDIN (CH.) . . . . Paris

ON THE COAST OF BRITTANY
20 x 30

5

ELIOT (MAURICE) . . . . . . Paris

Monet's Best Pupil

IN THE DEPTHS OF THE WOODS
21 x 29

6

B. S. 1839

FLOWERS
19 x 24

7

BOGGS (F. M.) . . . . . New York

Silver Medal Universelle Exposition, 1889; Hors Concours

"PORT OF HAVRE"
25⅝ x 20

8

LESREL (A.) . . . . Paris

HAPPY MOMENTS
18 x 13

9

FOUACE (LEON) . . . . . . Paris

STILL LIFE
25½ x 20

10

FUECHSEL (H) . . . . . New York

CROTONDALE ON THE HUDSON
32 x 22

11

DUPRE (JULIEN) . . . . . . Paris
Born at Nantes, 1812
Medal, 1833; Cross of the Legion of Honor, 1849;
Medal, 1867; Exposition Universelle; Officer of
the Legion of Honor, 1870; Hors Concours

RETURNING FROM THE FIELDS
15 x 21

12

DENNENLIN (JULES) . . . . . Paris
Medal, 1875

FROG FISHING
22⅛ x 30

MONCHABLON (ALPHONSE)   Paris

Born at Avillais (Vosges)
Pupil of Cornu and Gleyre
Hors Concours

"VALLEY OF ENFOUELLE, VOSGES"

9⅝ x 13¾

14

STEVENS (ALFRED) . . . . . Paris

Born at Brussels
Medal, 1853, 1855, 1863, 1867, 1878; Grand Prix, 1889;
Hors Concours

VIEW OF BORDIGHERA

12¾ x 16⅛

15

HAGBORG (A.) . . . . Paris

Medal, 1879; Legion of Honor, 1879;
Hors Concours

WATCHING FOR RETURN OF BOATS

21 x 16

16

ROUGERON (J.) . . . . . . Paris

A WELCOME LETTER

17 x 25

17

WASHINGTON (GEORGES) . . . . Paris

Born at Marseilles
Medal, Third Class, 1893

HORSES IN A POOL

23¾ x 31⅝

18

De CAMPS (ALEX. G.) ; dec'd . . . . Paris

Born in Paris, 1803; died at Fontainebleau, 1860
Pupil of Abel de Pujol, David and Ingres

AT THE SPRING

10 x 16

19

LEWIN (STEPHEN) . . . . . London

WHITEBAIT AT GREENWICH

35 x 43

20

GRANT (C. R.) . . . . . New York

THE HOME OF EVANGELINE

26 x 36

21
JETTEL (EUGENE) . . . . .

Pupil of Academy at Vienna and Theodore Rousseau
Member of Societé Nationale des Beaux-Arts; Member
of the Jury Exposition Universelle, 1889; Chevalier of the Legion of Honor; First Class Medal,
International Exposition, Munich, 1891

HORSES NEAR A CANAL

26 x 17½

22
WILLEMS (FLORENT) . . . .

Medals, Paris 1844, 1846, 1855, 1867, 1878; Legion of
Honor, 1853; Officer, 1864; Commander, 1878

FLIRTATION

18 x 21½

23
JONGKIND (J. B.) . . . . . Holland

Born at Lathrop, Holland, 1822
Pupil of Isabey
Medal, 1852. Exempt

ON THE CANAL

13 x 18

24
BINET (A.) . . . . Paris

LANDSCAPE AND CATTLE

22 x 32

25

CARRADINI (C.) . . . . . Rome

THE CARDINAL'S VISIT
18 x 27

26

VOIGT (A) . . . . Paris

LANDSCAPE AND CATTLE
22 x 33

27

SCHENCK (AUG.) . . . . . . Paris

Born at Gluckstadt (Holstein), 1828
Pupil of L. Cogniet
Medals, Paris Salon, 1865; Legion of Honor, 1888;
Chevalier of the Order of Christ of Portugal;
Chevalier of the Order of Isabella La Catholica;
Medal, Centennial Exhibition, 1876

SHEEP IN A SNOWSTORM
15⅝ x 19¾

28

McCORD (GEO. H.) . . . . New York

A. N. A.

SUNSET AT GLOUCESTER
24 x 36

MICHEL (GEORGES); dec'd . . . . Paris

Born at Paris, 1763; died, 1843.

Studied the art of the Dutch master, Van Goyan, closely,
whose style he painted, but with more strength
and less delicacy. His early pictures display a cer-
tain richness of color and elaboration of detail,
but in his later and finer style he simplified his
system, and produced those massive compositions,
vast plains and solid hills, under skies quivering
with exquisite grays and rolling with storm,
through which he has become to his country
what Constable was to England. He left all his
pictures unsigned, because, as he said, there was
but one Michel, and would not be another

CLOUDY DAY

22 x 35

30

MONTICELLI (A.); dec'd . . . . Paris

Born at Marseilles, 1824; died, 1886
Pupil of Raymond Aubert and of Diaz

GARDEN PARTY

8 x 18

31

DIAZ (N. V.); dec'd . . . . . . Paris

Born at Bordeaux, 1807; died, 1876
Medals, 1844, 1846, 1848; Legion of Honor, 1851;
Diploma to the Memory of Deceased Artists,
Universal Exhibition, 1878

IN THE QUIET OF THE WOODS

14 x 17

ROYBET (F.) . . . . Paris

Born at Uzes, 1840
Pupil of Vibert and l'ecole des Beaux-Arts.
Medal, 1866

"IDEAL HEAD"
(Study)
19 x 24

33

ROUSSEAU (TH.); dec'd . . . . . Paris

Medals, 1834, 1849, 1855; Legion of Honor, 1852;
one of the eight Grand Medals of Honor, Exposition Universelle, Paris, 1867; Diploma to
Memory of Deceased Artists, 1868

PEN AND INK DRAWING
14 x 24

34

DETTI (CESARE) . . . . . . Paris

Medal, Brussels, 1889; E. U. Silver Medal, 1889;
E. U. Medal, Second Class; Hors Concours

THE KING'S PAGE
18 x 21½

35

CHAIGNEAU (F.) . . . . . . Paris

Born in Bordeaux
Medal, 1889

EWE AND LAMB
11½ x 12½

ZIEM (FELIX) . . . . Paris

Born at Beaume (Cote d'Or), 1822
Studied at Paris
Medals, 1851, and First Class, 1852, Exposition Uni-
verselle; Cross of the Legion of Honor, 1852;
Officer of the Legion of Honor, 1878; Hors
Concours
This artist is celebrated for his gorgeous representa-
tions of Venice

VENICE

27 x 43

MAUVE (ANTON) . . . . . Holland

Born at Zaamdam, Holland
Pupil of Van Oos
Medals at Amsterdam, Antwerp, Brussels, and The
Hague

LANDSCAPE AND CATTLE

25 x 13

DESGOFFE (BLAISE) . . . . . Paris

Still Life Painter
Pupil of Flandrau
Medals, 1861, 1863

" Desgoffe, the painter of still life, for thorough Imitation of
jewels, tapestries, objects of art, and precious things in gen-
eral,—he never wastes time on vulgar things,—excels even
Dutchmen. Perfect in design, truthful in color, finished to
microscopic exactness of detail, he leaves the spectator
nothing to desire in these respects."—*Jarves' "Art
Thoughts."*

"OBJETS d'ART"

WORMS (JULES) . . . . . . Paris

Born at Paris, 1837
Pupil of Lafosse
Medals, 1867, 1868, and 1869; Cross of the Legion of
Honor, 1876. Medal, 1878, Exposition Univer-
selle. Hors Concours. This artist's picture of
"Romance a la Mode" is in the Luxembourg

THE TWO ORPHANS

13 x 17

JACQUE (CHAS. EMILE); dec'd . . Paris

Born at Paris, 1813
First President of the French Society of Animal
Painters
For Designs, Medals, 1851, 1861, and 1863; Cross of
the Legion of Honor, 1867; Medal, 1867, Exposition Universelle; for Paintings, Medals, 1861,
1863 and 1864; Hors Concours

LANDSCAPE AND SHEEP

DAUBIGNY (C. F.); dec'd . . . . Paris

Pupil of his father and of Paul Delaroche
Medals, 1848, 1853, 1855, 1857, 1859, 1867; Legion of
Honor, 1858; Exposition Universelle, 1878; Officer
of the Legion of Honor, 1874; Diploma to the
Memory of Deceased Artists

ON THE BANKS OF THE OISE

42

SEMENOWSKY (EISMAN) . . .

ARRANGING THE FLOWERS

11 x 34

43

WASSERMAN . . . . . .

THE CONVALESCENT

13 x 16

44

COROT (J. B. C.); dec'd . . . . . Paris

Born in Paris, 1809; died, 1875
Pupil of Michallon and Victor Bertin
Medals, 1833; First Class, 1848, 1855; Cross of the
Legion of Honor, 1846; Medal, Universal Exposi-
tion, 1877; Officer of the Legion of Honor, 1867;
Hors Concours; Diploma to the Memory of De-
ceased Artists, 1878, Exposition Universelle

LANDSCAPE

45

CASANOVA Y ESTORACH (A.); dec'd, Madrid

Born in Tortosa, Spain, August 3d, 1847; died, 1897
Pupil of J. Sabater and of the Academy of Fine Arts
of Barcelona
H. M., Madrid, 1866; Prix de Rome, 1870; medals,
1876, 1877, 1878 and 1879; Hors Concours

LAID UP FOR REPAIRS

15 x 18

TROYON (CONSTANTINE); dec'd . . Paris

Born at Sevres, 1810; died, 1865
His parents wished him to be a painter of porcelain,
but after a time spent in the manufactory at Sevres
he studied under Riocreux, and became a painter
of landscape and animals
Medals, Paris, 1838, 1840, 1846, 1848, 1855; Legion of
Honor, 1849; Member of the Amsterdam Academy; Diploma to the Memory of Deceased
Artists; Exposition Universelle, 1878

LANDSCAPE AND CATTLE

47

TER MEULEN . . . . . The Hague

Pupil of Mauve

HOME FROM THE PASTURE
40 x 29

48

ELIOT (MAURICE) . . . . . . Paris

Pupil of Monet

LANDSCAPE
21 x 28½

49

HART (WM.) . . . . . New York

N. A.

EARLY SUMMER
9 x 14

50

BERAUD (L.) . . . . Paris

ENTRANCE TO GRAND HALL OF
THE LOUVRE

13 x 16

51

HART (WM.); dec'd . . . . New York

N. A.

THE MEADOWS

6¼ x 12½

52

ROUSSEAU (TH.); dec'd . . . . . Paris

Born in Paris, 1812; died 1897
Pupil of Guillon-Letheiere. First exhibited at the Salon
in 1834. Medals, 1834, 1840, 1855; Legion of
Honor, 1852; one of the eight Grand Medals of
Honor, E. U., Paris, 1867

LANDSCAPE, SUNSET

8½ x 7½

53

WOOD (THOS. W.) . . . . New York

A. N. A.

THE LAST RESORT

14 x 20

SHEWIN (D.) . . . . . . London

RURAL ENGLAND
40 x 20

55

DUPRE (JULES); /dec'd . . . . Paris

Born at Nantes, 1812
Medal, 1833; Cross of the Legion of Honor, 1849;
Medal, 1867, Exposition Universelle; Officer of
the Legion of Honor, 1870; Hors Concours

LANDSCAPE
23 x 17

56

BRUNIN (LEON) . . . . . . Paris

THE PROPOSAL
31 x 39

57

JONGKIND (J. B.) . . . . . Holland

Born at Lathrop, Holland, 1822
Pupil of Isabey
Medal, 1852; exempt

" MOONLIGHT "
15 x 18

59   THE SCOLDING WIFE.   J. Meadow.

58

WOODWELL (JOSEPH R.) . . New York

AUTUMN, NEW ENGLAND COAST

32 x 24

59

MADOU (J.); dec'd . . . . . Brussels

Born January 26, 1796; died April 3, 1877
Pupil of P. J. C. Francois

THE SCOLDING WIFE
(From the Crabbe collection)

21½ x 29½

60

MARCOTTE de QUIVIERES (AUG. M. PAUL)

. . . . Paris

Honorable mention, 1886 and 1889

FISHING BOATS, EARLY MORNING
OFF DIEPPE

32 x 21⅜

LANDSCAPE AND CATTLE

SECOND EVENING, FRIDAY, MARCH 17th

8 O'CLOCK

❦

61

DELACHAUX (LEON) . . . . . Paris

24⅝ x 30⅛

ALWAYS SPEAK THE TRUTH

62

IRELAND (THOMAS) . . . . London

ON THE THAMES

63

WAHLBERG (ALFRED) . . . Stockholm

Medal, 1870, Second Class, 1872; Legion of Honor,
1874; Medal, First Class, 1878; Hors Concours

AT SUNDOWN

18¼ x 29¼

64

LAUGEE (GEO.) . . . . . . Paris

Medals, 1881, 1889; Hors Concours

HOME LIFE IN THE FIELDS

33 x 27

RICHET (LEON) . . . . Paris

Born at Solesmes (Nord)
Pupil of Diaz, Lefebere and Boulanger
Honorable Mention, 1885

NEAR FONTAINEBLEAU

18¼ x 24

MILLET (JEAN FRANCOIS); dec'd . . Paris

Born at Greville (Manche), October 4, 1814; died at
Barbizon (Seine-et-Marne), January 20, 1875
Pupil of Mouchel, Langlots and Delaroche
His best work began in 1849, with contributions to
the Salon, and continued up to 1870. A peasant
himself in origin, his representations of peasant
life, with simple, earnest feeling and a comprehen-
sion of its pathos, was such as no other painter has
reached. In 1889 his " Angelus " was sold to the
American Art Association for 553,000 frs., and
they sold it afterward to M. Chauchard, of Paris,
for 750,000 frs. All his works command very
high prices

RETURN FROM MARKET

LESREL (A.) . . . . Paris

FRIENDLY COMPETITORS

13 x 17½

68

WASSERMAN . . . .

A MORNING CALL
13 x 16

69

DAUBIGNY (C. F.) ; dec'd . . . . Paris

Born at Paris, 1817 ; died, 1878
Pupil of Paul Delaroche
Medals, 1848, 1853, 1855, 1857, 1859, 1867 ; Legion of
Honor, 1874 ; Diploma to the Memory of Deceased
Artists ; Exposition Universelle, 1878

ON THE BANKS OF THE MARNE

70

VERHAS (JAN.) . . . . . Brussels

Medals at Philadelphia, Brussels, Paris, Vienna and Ber-
lin ; Legion of Honor, 1888

MAY I COME IN?
26 x 39

71

COROT (J. B. C.) ; dec'd . . . . . Paris

Born in Paris, 1796 ; died 1875
Pupil of Michallon and Bertin
Medals. Paris, 1838, 1848, 1855, and Exposition Universelle, 1867 ; Legion of Honor, 1846 ; Officer of
the Legion of Honor, 1867 ; Diploma to the
Memory of Deceased Artists, Exposition Universelle, 1878

LANDSCAPE
18 x 13

STEINHEIL (ALBERT) . . . . . Paris

Medal, Third Class, 1882; bronze medal, Universelle
Exposition; Hors Concours

AMATEUR OF PAINTING
15 x 18

WAHLBERG (A. L.) . . . . . . Paris

Born in Stockholm, Sweden
Pupil of Corot
Medals, Paris, 1870, 1872, and 1878; Legion of Honor,
1874; Officer of the Legion of Honor, 1879

ON THE RIVER, MOONLIGHT
36 x 24

PERRAULT (LEON) . . . . . Paris

Medals, Paris, 1864, 1876, 1889; Legion of Honor, 1887
Hors Concours

SUNNY ITALY
13 x 16

MONTICELLI (A.) ; dec'd . . . . . Paris

Born, 1824; died, 1886
Pupil of Aubert

LANDSCAPE
22 x 29

76

ESCOSURA (IGNACE de LEON) . . . Spain

Born at Oviedo, Spain
Pupil of Gérôme

LOOKING AT THE JEWELS

9 x 12

77

PERRAULT (LEON) . . . . . . Paris

Medals, Paris, 1864, 1876, 1889, E. U.; Chevalier of the
Legion of Honor, 1887; Hors Concours

INNOCENCE

78

BLINKS (THOS.) . . . . . London

R. A.

A GOOD STAND

79

DE VRINDT (ALBRECHT) . . . Antwerp

Pupil of Baron Leys

OF THE HOUSEHOLD OF CHARLEMAGNE

ZIEM (FELIX) . . . . Paris

Born at Beaume (Côte d'Or), 1832
Medals, 1851, 1852, 1855, Exposition Universelle;
Cross of the Legion of Honor, 1857; Officer of
the Legion of Honor, 1878; Hors Concours

IN FRONT OF VENICE

81

BLINKS (THOS.) R. A., ... London

IN CHARGE

82

DETTI (CESARE) . . . . . . Paris

Medal, Brussels, 1889; E. U. Silver Medal, 1889;
E. U. Medal, Second Class; Hors Concours

A BOATING PARTY

83

ROYBET (F.) . . . . Paris

Born at Uzes, 1840
Pupil of Vibert, l'Ecole des Beaux Arts
Medal, 1866

CHEVALIER OF THE SIXTEENTH CENTURY.
(From the Crabbe Collection)

22 x 15

36

IN FRONT OF VENICE.

FELIX ZIEM.

84

VELY (ANATOLE) . . . . . . Paris

THE FIRST STEP

46½ x 74

85 ·

GEROME (J. L.) . . . . . . Paris

Medals, Paris 1847, 1848, 1855; Exhibition Universelle ;
Medal of the Institute, 1865; Medal of Honor (E.
U.), 1867, 1874; Medal for Sculpture and one of
the Eight Grand Medals of Honor, 1855; Officer
of the Legion of Honor, 1867; Commander of the
Legion of Honor, 1878; Chevalier of the Ordre
del Aigle Rouge and Member of the Institute of
France, 1878; Professor in l'Ecole des Beaux Arts

NOONDAY REST

26 x 17½

86

MAUVE (ANTON); dec'd . . The Hague

Born in Saandau, Holland
Pupil of Van Oos
Medals, Amsterdam, Antwerp, Brussels and The Hague

LANDSCAPE AND SHEEP, MOONLIGHT

24 x 19

85   J. L. Gerome.

NOONDAY REST.

87

TROYON (CONSTANTINE); dec'd . . Paris

Born at Sevres, 1810; died, 1865
His parents wished him to be a painter of porcelain,
but after a time spent in the manufactory at
Sevres he studied under Riocreux, and became a
painter of landscape and animals
Medals, Paris, 1838, 1840, 1846, 1848, 1855; Legion of
Honor, 1849; Member of the Amsterdam Acad-
emy; Diploma to the Memory of Deceased Artists;
Exposition Universelle, 1878

LANDSCAPE AND CATTLE

88

VAN MARCKE (EMIL); dec'd . . . Paris

Born at Sevres (Seine-et-Oise)
Pupil and son-in-law of Troyon
Medals, 1867, 1869, 1870; Cross of the Legion of
Honor, 1872; Medals of the First Class, 1878, Ex-
position Universelle; Hors Concours

AT THE BROOK

21½ x 28½

89

JACQUE (CHAS. EMILE) . . . . . Paris

Born at Paris, 1813
First President of the French Society of Animal
Painters; for Designs, Medals, 1851, 1861 and
1863; Cross of the Legion of Honor, 1867; Medal,
1867, Exposition Universelle; for Paintings,
Medals, 1861, 1863 and 1864; Hors Concours

LANDSCAPE WITH SHEEP

20 x 25

DAUBIGNY (C. F.); dec'd . . . . . . Paris

Born at Paris, 1817; died, 1878
Pupil of Paul Delaroche
Medals, 1848, 1853, 1855, 1857, 1859, 1867; Legion of
Honor, 1894; Diploma to the Memory of De-
ceased Artists; Exposition Universelle, 1878

ON THE SEINE

91

SCHREYER (AD.) . . . . . . Paris

Born at Frankfort, 1828
Pupil of Stadel Institute
Medals, 1864, 1865, 1867; Court Painter to the Grand
Duke of Mecklenburg, 1862; Medal, Brussels,
1863; Chevalier of the Order of Leopold, 1866;
Medal, Vienna, 1873; Medal, Munich, 1876; Mem-
ber of the Academies of Antwerp and Rotterdam

ON THE ALERT

26¼ x 32⅜

92

ROUSSEAU (TH.); dec'd . . . . . . Paris

Born at Paris, 1812; died, 1897
Pupil of Guillon-Letheiere.
First exhibited at the Salon in 1834. Medals, 1834,
1840, 1855; Legion of Honor, 1852; one of the
eight Grand Medals of Honor, E. U., Paris, 1867
(From the celebrated Arthur Stevens collection)

SUNSET TINTS

7 x 10

ISRAELS (JOSEF) . . . . .

In a letter accompanying the painting, Mr. Israel says:
" The picture is one of my early works. I painted
it about the year 1853, and had much pleasure
from it, as it was a success in the Amsterdam
Exhibition of that year. It has been engraved
by Taurel and others."

MEDITATION

54 x 83

HOBBEMA (MEYNDERT); dec'd . Amsterdam

Born 1638; died at Amsterdam, 1709
Studied under Jacob Van Ruisdael. Much neglected
in his lifetime, Hobbema now takes rank as one
of the greatest masters of landscape painting

LANDSCAPE

22 x 28

DIAZ (N. V.); dec'd . . . . . . Paris

Died, 1876
Medals, 1844, 1846, 1848; Legion of Honor, 1851;
Diploma of Honor in Memoriam; Exposition
Universelle, 1878

FLOWERS

21 x 28

96

COROT (J. B. C.); dec'd . . . . . **Paris**

Born at Paris, 1796; died, 1875
Pupil of Bertin
Medals, Paris, 1838, 1848, 1855, and Exposition Universelle, 1867; Legion of Honor, 1846; Officer of the Legion of Honor, 1867; Diploma to the Memory of Deceased Artists, Exposition Universelle, 1878

LANDSCAPE

97

HOWE (W. H.) . . . . . **New York**

Pupil of Von Thoren and Mauve

LANDSCAPE AND CATTLE
18 x 12

98

HAQUETTE (GEORGES) . . . . **Paris**

Born at Paris
Pupil of Millet and Cabanel
Medals, Paris Salon, 1880; Boston, 1883. Nice, 1884; Member of the Society of French Artists; his painting entitled "The Departure" was purchased by the French Government, and presented to the City of Dieppe.

THE HELPING HAND
39½ x 28⅞

MULLER (R. G.); dec'd . . . . Munich

OLD MOORISH GATEWAY, TANGIERS
24 x 36

INNESS (GEORGE); dec'd . . New York

Born, 1825; died, 1894
Member of National Academy of Design

SUNBURST
20 x 30

KAEMMERER (FRED HENRI) . . . Paris

Born at Haye
Medals, Third Class, 1874, 1889; Hors Concours

RAIN
10⅜ x 18⅛

HASSAM (CHILDE) . . . . New York

STREET SCENES, PARIS

103

DUPRE (JULES); dec'd . . . . . Paris

Born at Nantes, 1811 ; died, 1889
Medals, 1833, 1867; Legion of Honor 1849; Officer of
the Legion of Honor, 1870

MARINE

6 x 12

104

BERNE-BELLECOUR (E.) . . . . Paris

Born at Boulogne-sur-Mer ; (pas de Calais)
Pupil of Picot and Barrias
Medal, 1869 ; Medals, First Class, 1872, 1878 ; Cross of
the Legion of Honor, 1878 ; Medal, 1889, Exposition Universelle ; Hors Concours

DINNER TIME

16 x 23

105

THOREN (OTTO VON) . . . . Paris

Medals

LANDSCAPE AND CATTLE

106

BLOMMERS (B. T.) . . . . . Holland

Pupil of Israels
Various medals

AT THE SEASIDE

22 x 31

107

MICHEL (GEORGES); dec'd . . . . **Paris**

Represented in the Louvre at Paris

AFTER THE SHOWER

22 x 35

108

FICHEL (E.) . . . . **Paris**

Medals, 1857, 1861, 1869; Legion of Honor, 1870;
Hors Concours.

HALL OF THE GUARDS

15 x 22

109

JONGKIND (J. B.) . . . . . **Holland**

Born at Lathrop, Holland, 1822
Pupil of Isabey
Medal, 1852; Exempt

SUNSET ON THE BANKS OF THE CANAL

18 x 21½

110

OOST (JACOB VAN) . . . . **Bruges**

The Younger, born, 1639; died, 1713

PORTRAIT OF A LADY

25⅛ x 38¼

111

MONTICELLI (A.); dec'd . . . . . . Paris

Born, 1824; died, 1886
Pupil of Aubert

LANDSCAPE WITH FIGURES

112

TENIERS (DAVID) . . . . .

Born in 1610; died, 1690

VILLAGE SCENE

4 x 6

113

SIMONOWSKY (EISMAN) . . .

Pupil of Van Beers

HIDE AND GO SEEK

22½ x 34

114

HENNER (J. J.) . . . . . . Paris

Medals, Paris, 1858, 1863, 1865, 1866; Legion of
Honor, 1873; Officer of the Legion of Honor,
1878; Hors Concours

IDEAL HEAD

16 x 21

VIBERT (J. G.) . . . . Paris

Medals, 1864, 1867, 1868, 1878; Legion of Honor,
1870; Officer of the Legion of Honor, 1882;
Medal, Third Class, 1878, Universal Exposition;
Hors Concours

A VISIT TO THE BARBER'S

8 x 11

116

BOUGUEREAU (MRS. E) . . . . Paris

(Miss Elizabeth Gardner)

EASTER LILIES

117

GAY (WM. ALLEN) . . . . . Boston

Pupil of Diaz

THE PALACE MOAT, TOKIO, JAPAN

118

NORTON (W. E.) . . . . . London

MOONLIGHT ON THE THAMES

This painting was exhibited in the Paris Salon, and
awarded "Honorable Mention." It was exhibited
at the recent World's Fair, Omaha

119

HART (WM.) . . . . . New York

Born, 1822; died, 1894

N. A., 1858; Vice President Academy of Design; President W. C. Society, 1870 to 1873

APPLE BLOSSOMS

10 x 14¼

www.ingramcontent.com/pod-product-compliance
Lightning Source LLC
Chambersburg PA
CBHW021549270326
41930CB00008B/1428